MW01028918

Newfoundland
Recipes

Carol Over

St. John's, Newfoundland

© 1979, Carol Over

Cover Art and Design: Kevin Tobin

∞ Printed on acid-free paper

Printing History:

First Printing — March 1979
Second Printing — May 1979
Third Printing — June 1979
Fourth Printing — August 1979
Fifth Printing — November 1979
Sixth Printing — February 1980
Seventh Printing — May 1980
Eighth Printing — July 1980
Ninth Printing — June 1981
Tenth Printing — September 1981
Eleventh Printing — April 1982
Twelfth Printing — June 1982
Thirteenth Printing — August 1982
Fourteenth Printing — November 1982
Fifteenth Printing — June 1983
Sixteenth Printing — June 1984

Seventeenth Printing — May 1985
Eighteenth Printing — June 1986
Nineteenth Printing — August 1986
Twentieth Printing — April 1987
Twenty-first Printing — July 1987
Twenty-second Printing — July 1989
Twenty-third Printing — April 1991
Twenty-fourth Printing — August 1992
Twenty-fifth Printing — August 1994
Twenty-sixth Printing — May 1996
Twenty-seventh Printing — June 1997
Twenty-eighth Printing — November 1998
Twenty-ninth Printing — January 2000
Thirtieth Printing — April 2001
Thirty-first Printing — April 2002

Published by
CREATIVE BOOK PUBLISHING
a division of 10366 Newfoundland Limited
a Robinson-Blackmore Printing & Publishing associated company
P.O. Box 8660, St. John's, Newfoundland A1B 3T7
ph. (709) 722-8500   fax. (709) 722-2228
email: books@rb.nf.ca   URL: www.nfbooks.com

Printed in Canada by:
ROBINSON-BLACKMORE PRINTING & PUBLISHING

ISBN 0-920021-69-7

FOREWORD

This book of "Newfoundland Recipes" contains a delightful variety of taste-tempting dishes from the kitchens of Newfoundland. I am sure you will find it a helpful reference in the preparation of meals which are sure to please those who enjoy good Newfoundland cooking. I wish you many enjoyable hours of cooking and baking.

—Carol J. Over

Contents

Main Dishes

Salads

Breads and Rolls

Desserts

Beverages

———

Main dishes

Pea Soup

2 cups split peas
1 onion, chopped
1 cup celery, diced
1 cup potato, diced
½ turnip, diced
3 carrots, diced
1 pound salt meat or ham bone

Soak salt meat and peas overnight. Drain off water.
Add 6 cups of water and onion. Simmer gently for 3
hours. About 20 minutes before serving, add
vegetables. If soup is too thick add extra water. Make
doughboys as follows: 1½ cups flour, ¼ cup butter, 3
teaspoons baking powder, 1 teaspoon salt, ½ to ¾ cup
water or milk. Cut butter into small pieces in the flour,
baking powder and salt. Add water or milk to make a
soft dough. Drop by teaspoonfuls into soup. Cover pot
tightly and cook for 15 minutes.

Mrs. Elsie Vokey
Gander

Baked Herring

4 herring, gutted and stuffed. Leave herring round if possible, remove gut and head. Stuffing: 2 slices of bread, crumbled fine; onion to taste; pinch of savory; one tablespoon of melted butter.

Stuff herring, secure top of herring with skewer. Cut fat pork in about 1½ inch pieces in length, place on bottom of roasting pan, lay herring on top of pork, then place pork same size on top of herring. Bake in 325° oven for 4 hours, remove cover and bake for another 30 minutes.

Mrs. Marion Abbott
Springdale

Creamed Codfish

Ingredients:

2 cups cooked codfish (fresh, frozen, tinned or salted)
4 tbsp. butter or margarine
4 tbsp. flour
3 cups milk
pepper
salt

Method: Melt butter or margarine in top of double boiler, blend in flour, add milk gradually and cook, stirring constantly until sauce thickens. Add flaked fish. Add salt and pepper to taste. Heat and serve on toast, hot baking powder biscuits or over broiled potatoes.

Priscilla March
Lady Cove

Seafood Casserole

½ cup butter
1½ tablespoons flour
1½ cups milk
1 pound cod fillets (cut in bite-size pieces)
1 can medium-size shrimp drained
1 teaspoon chopped parsley
1 small can sliced mushrooms (drained)
3 raw potatoes sliced

Melt butter in a saucepan, add onions and cook until soft. Remove from heat. Stir in flour, add milk and return to heat. Cook, stirring constantly until thickened and smooth. Arrange cod and shrimp in a buttered casserole dish. Sprinkle with parsley and mushrooms. Pour half of sauce over fish. Top with layers of sliced potatoes and pour remaining sauce over casserole. Bake for 40 minutes in a 375° oven or until potatoes are tender.

Mrs. Muriel Faulken
Gander

Fried Cod Tongues

1½ cups flour
1 teaspoon salt
½ teaspoon pepper
7 to 8 cod tongues per person
½ pound salt pork

Carefully wash cod tongues and dry in a paper towel. Mix together flour, salt and pepper in a plastic bag. Shake tongues in the mixture until evenly coated. Fry salt pork until golden brown. Remove pork cubes and fry tongues in same pan. Cook until golden brown on both sides. Serve with mashed potatoes and green peas.

Mrs. Effie Adams
Springdale

3

Sam Huxter's
Bake-Pot Salmon

1 fresh salmon (3-4 lbs)
2 large onions, sliced
2 tablespoons water
½ pound salt pork
6 medium potatoes
salt and pepper

Cut salmon in 1 inch slices. Spread slices of pork on bottom of pot. Cook 5 minutes, add cut salmon, onions, sliced potatoes all at one time, making sure the salmon is on the bottom. Shake salt and pepper over all. Add 2 tablespoons of water, simmer for two hours. An iron pot gives the best results.

Mrs. Marion Abbott
Springdale

Baked Stuffed Squid

6 squid
1 teaspoon poultry seasoning
2 teaspoons melted butter
2 cups bread crumbs
½ teaspoon salt
1 onion chopped

Clean squid by removing tentacles and skin. Wash thoroughly and sprinkle with salt. Make a dressing by combining poultry seasoning, butter, crumbs & onion. Stuff the squid, adding strips of fat pork to each squid. Place the squid on skewers and sew the ends. Wrap in aluminum foil and bake for ¾ hour in a 350° oven.

Mrs. Olive Paul
Bonavista

4

Friday Casserole

½ cup melted margarine
3 cups coarsely ground carrot
1 cup finely cut celery
1 cup soft bread crumbs
1 med onion, finely chopped
1 cup cubed farmers cheese
½ tsp. salt
2 beaten eggs
½ cup chopped nuts

Mix all ingredients together, bake in greased covered dish at 350° for 40 minutes. Uncover and bake an additional 8 minutes.

Mrs. H. Budgell
St. John's

Nfld. Tuna Casserole

2 cups medium noodles
1 10 oz. can cream of celery soup
1 tablespoon soya sauce
½ cup Carnation milk
2 tablespoons Good Luck
1 cup finely chopped celery
½ cup finely chopped onion
½ small garlic, minced
1 dash tabasca sauce
1½ to 2 lbs. Newfoundland tuna, cooked and broken into large pieces
½ cup chopped salted peanuts.

Heat oven 350 degrees. Butter a 1½ quart casserole dish. Cook noodles and drain. Combine soup, soya sauce, tabasco and Carnation milk. Heat Good Luck in small skillet and add celery, onion, and garlic, cooking gently until onion is yellow. Add to soup mixture. Combine soup mixture with Cooked noodles and peanuts blending lightly. Spoon into prepared casserole dish and bake 30 to 40 minutes or until bubbling well. Serves 4 to 6.

May Budgell
Windsor

5

Baked Cod Fish

Choose a firm codfish. Remove head, tail and soundbone. Wash and clean skin with a sharp knife. Wipe dry.

DRESSING:
3 cups soft bread crumbs
1 tablespoon grated onion
1 tablespoon savoury
1 teaspoon salt
⅛ teaspoon pepper
3 tablespoons butter

Mix dressing ingredients together and stuff the fish. Tie securely on skewer. Place dressed fish in a roasting pan in which salt pork has been fried. Bake for 10 minutes in a 450° oven. Reduce heat to 400° and continue baking for 1 hour. Baste occasionally and add sliced onion during final 20 minutes of baking time.

Joyce Smith
Little Heart's Ease
Trinity Bay

Deep Fried Squid Rings

Clean squid and parboil for five minutes. Cut into rings and dip into batter.
Batter:
1 cup flour
1 teaspoon baking powder
1 teaspoon salt
1 egg
Combine ingredients, adding milk enough to make batter smooth.
After dipping rings, drop into hot fat and cook until golden brown.

Mrs. N. Riggs
Glovertown

Savoury Fish Cakes

2 pounds fresh or salt cod fish (boiled)
8 medium boiled potatoes (mashed)
1 medium diced onion
¼ cup flour
¼ pack savoury
Small piece of salt pork.

Cut salt pork into small pieces and fry until brown in frying pan. Remove pork cubes, leaving fat in pan to fry fish cakes.
Mix fish, potatoes, onion and savoury together. Shape into fish cakes and coat with flour. Fry on both sides until golden brown.

Mrs. Blanche Ryan
Port Rexton
Trinity Bay

Cod Fish Casserole

4 tablespoons butter
2 tablespoons flour
1 teaspoon salt
½ teaspoon pepper
2 cups milk
2½ cups fresh cooked codfish (flaked and cooled)
1 cup grated cheese

In a medium saucepan, melt butter and add flour, salt and pepper. Stir to make a paste. Add salt and cook until it thickens, stirring constantly. Grease a 2 quart casserole dish and pour a small amount of the sauce in the casserole dish. Add a layer of codfish and sprinkle with cheese. Repeat layers until all ingredients are used, topping casserole with a sprinkling of cheese. Bake for 30 minutes or until nicely browned in a 350° oven.

Mrs. Ann Russell
Clarenville
Trinity Bay

Boiled Salmon with Cream Sauce

Place salmon in pot. Cover with water, using pot small as possible. Add 1 teaspoon salt to each pound of salmon and ½ cup of white vinegar. Boil slowly for 20 minutes to each pound. Drain and skin.

Sauce
2 cups of fresh milk or 1 cup of canned milk and 1 cup of water, ½ teaspoon salt, 1 tablespoon corn flour, mix in a little cold water. Add to milk and boil. Add 1 tablespoon margarine and 1 hard boiled egg, chopped. Serve with Salmon and desired vegetables.

Minnie B. Small
Lewisporte

Salmon Supper Casserole

2 cups cooked salmon
1 large onion
4 medium sized potatoes
Salt and Pepper
1 cup milk
Flour

Remove bones and flake the fish. Spread one half the amount in buttered casserole. Cover with thin slices of onion and a generous layer of sliced raw potatoes. Sprinkle with salt and pepper and dredge with flour. Repeat these three layers then pour in milk. Dot with butter and bake at 400°F for about 50 minutes or until potatoes are tender.

Loretta Sullivan
Riverhead
Harbour Grace

Baked Moose Liver and Bacon

You will need —
six slices of moose liver
six slices of bacon,
1 small onion
seasoning to taste
1 ounce lard

Cooking time — 1 hour
Oven setting — 300° F.
Method: Line a baking tin with foil, leaving enough over to fold over the top, completely covering the contents. Lay one slice of bacon on each slice of liver and roll up together with a little chopped onion. Put about an ounce of fat on the foil in the bottom of the tin, and sprinkle in the rest of the onion. Place the six rolls in the tin and fold the foil over the top leaving both ends open but slightly turned upwards. Place in centre of oven and bake for 1 hour. Serve with any vegetables.

Eileen Spurrell
Pool's Island
Bonavista Bay

Quick Lunch Recipe

Macroni
1 lb. hamburger meat.
1 small tin tomato sauce
1 onion
2 tablespoons brown sugar
Salt and pepper

Boil water, add macroni, let boil until cooked. Fry meat in frying pan until brown. Add diced onions, salt and pepper. Then add tomato sauce diluted with water or milk. Drain macroni, add meat mixture. Stir until meat is mixed through and serve.

Mrs. Patsy Rogers
Eastport

Newfoundland Flipper Pie

2 seal flippers
1 small turnip, cubed
3 carrots, sliced
2 onions, sliced
1 parsnip, sliced
2½ cups of water
1½ oz Screech
½lb fat back pork
2 tablespoons vinegar
salt & pepper to taste
DUMPLING PASTRY
1½ cups of flour
2 teaspoons of baking powder
Small pat of butter

Cut all fat and slag from flippers, place them in a deep dish and add enough boiling water to cover; add vinegar & set aside to cool, then wipe dry with paper towel and place in baking pan or large casserole dish. Add pepper & salt to taste, cover with sliced onions and sliced fat pork. Dribble the Screech over contents. Cover and bake in a 375 degree oven (pre-heated) for two hours.
Boil turnip, carrots & parsnip in 2½ cups of water for about 20 minutes. When ready place in baking dish along with flipper. Use vegetable water for gravy -- thicken with flour.
Make dumpling pastry and pat over flippers & vegetables. Cover and bake gently until pastry is done (about 15 minutes.)

Floss LeDrew
Pasadena,
Humber River

Fresh Cod Fish Dressed

Clean and skin a medium cod fish. Keep in shape.
Sprinkle with salt.
Prepare dressing:
   3 cups bread crumbs
   2 oz. fat back pork, chopped fine
   1 medium onion, chopped
   1 level teaspoon salt
   1 level teaspoon pepper
Mix together, fill fish and pin together with scewer.
Cover fish with pieces of salt pork. Place in oven and
bake 1½ hours at 325°.

Minnie B. Small
Lewisporte

Baked Cod Tongues

1 lb. cod tongues
cracker crumbs
2 or 3 small onions
3 tablespoons butter
milk to cover
½ teaspoon salt
1 teaspoon savory
pepper to taste

Wash and dry cod tongues. Put layer of tonues in a
buttered 8" casserole; cover with cracker crumbs,
sliced onions, salt, pepper and savory; dot with butter.
Add another layer of tongues and continue until all are
used. Have a layer of crumbs on top. Dot with butter,
cover with milk. Bake at 350° F. until tongues are
cooked (about 1¼ hours)

Goldie Stockley
Durrell

Flipper Pie

Flippers
Pastry
Vegetables (cut as for stew)
Potatoes (cooked saparately or with meat)

Soak flippers in cold water with 1 tablespoon baking
soda. Fat will turn white. Remove fat. Dredge flippers
in salted flour and fry until brown in rendered pork fat.
Add a little water and simmer until partly tender. Put
in roaster with onion and other desired vegetables,
seasoning and about 1 cup water. When cooked top with
pastry and bake at 425° until nicely browned, about 15-
20 minutes.

Marilyn Glavine
Bishop's Falls

Moose Cabbage Rolls

1 onion, chopped
1 pound ground, lean moosemeat
salt and pepper to taste
1 onion, grated
½ cup cooked rice
2 cups canned tomatoes (crushed)
2 tablespoons vinegar
2 tablespoons sugar
¼ teaspoon chili powder
8 large cabbage leaves.

Soften cabbage leaves in boiling water. Brown meat
and onion in pan. Season meat with salt and pepper,
add grated onion and cooked rice, mix well. Place a
large spoonful on cabbage leaf, roll, place them in a
kettle with rolled edge down or fasten ends with tooth-
picks. Add remaining ingredients and a little water.
Simmer or bake 1½ - 2 hours.

Marilyn Glavine
Bishop's Falls

Nfld. Pot Day
Tuesday or Thursday

1 package dried peas
3 pounds salt corned beef
1 head cabbage
1 turnip
6 potatoes
1 pound carrots

Soak beef in cold water overnight. Bring to a boil in the morning (10 a.m.) next, add cabbage and then turnip. When nearly cooked add whole potatoes and carrots. Place peas in a muslin bag and boil in water strained from the beef. When cooked, serve for noon meal.

Maureen Smith
Little Heart's Ease
Trinity Bay

Shepherd's Pie

1 medium onion
1 lb. ground beef
¾ teaspoon salt
dash of pepper
1 can green peas
1 can of condensed tomato soup
whipped potatoes

Chop onions and fry with ground beef, draining excess fat. Place meat and peas (drained) in a casserole dish and cover with whipped potatoes.
Whipped Potatoes:
5 medium potatoes, cooked
½ cup warm milk
1 egg, beaten
pinch salt
Mash potatoes when still hot, adding other ingredients. Place pie in a 350° oven and bake until browned.

Mrs. N. Riggs
Glovertown

13

Baked Stuffed Cod Fish

Cut up a piece of salt pork and place in large roaster. Then put roaster in oven to let pork render out its fat. Prepare medium sized fish by cleaning it thoroughly. Remove part of sound bone. Stuff fish with dressing below. Stitch together with thread or lacers.

Savory Dressing
2 cups bread crumbs
¼ cup butter or margarine (melted)
1 tablespoon savory
pepper and salt to taste
1 small onion (chopped)

Mix all ingredients together well.
Placed stuffed fish in roaster. Garnish top of fish with a few slices of salt pork. Place in a 350° oven for about 2½ hours or until done. Baste fish with pork drippings until browned. Then add about 1 cup of water and ½ hour before its done add medium sized onion.

Mrs. Daphne Over
Southern Bay

Meat Loaf

1 lb. mincemeat
1 egg
1½ teaspoons salt
½ cup finely chopped onions
1 cup milk
2 cups bread crumbs
1 teaspoon sage or savoury

Mix all ingredients together and turn into a well greased pan. Bake in 375° oven for 1 hour.

Mrs. James Kent
Bishop's Falls

Fishermen's Treat

8 large cabbage leaves
2 teasp. pork fat
½ lb. sausage meat
1 medium onion
2 cups tomatoes (Chop)
½ teasp. salt
pepper
1 tablespoon sugar
1½ cups cooked spaghetti

Cook cabbage leaves in boiling water for five minutes.
Drain. Heat fat and fry sausage meat and chopped
onions until brown. Add 1 cup chopped tomatoes, salt,
pepper, sugar and cooked spaghetti. Simmer and stir
until hot and well blended. Put a heaping teasp. on
cabbage leaf, roll up and fasten with toothpick. Put in a
baking dish, pour second cup of chopped tomatoes over
the roll. Cover and cook to 400 degrees for 30 min.
Remove cover and let brown. Serve with mashed
potatoes.

MaryAnn Hussey
19 Read St.
Gander

Baked Herring

6 fresh herring
Salt & pepper to taste
3 parts vinegar to 1 part water solution
Pickling spices.

Clean Herring by removing entrails, fins & scales. Cut
across the backs twice and place in a shallow baking
dish. Season with salt and pepper and cover with
vinegar/water solution. Sprinkle with pickling spices.
Cover and bake for 4 hours in a moderate oven.

Marilyn Glavine
Bishop's Falls

Turrs (Meal-in-a-Dish)

2 turrs
Preheat oven to 350°F
Toss together for stuffing.
4 slices of bread, cubed
1 apple, chopped
1 onion, chopped
½ teaspoon savoury
½ cup butter or margarine, melted.

Slice ½ pound salt pork.
Use half to line a baking dish. Place stuffed turrs on top and cover with remaining salt pork.
Bake in a covered dish in preheated oven for 1½ hours.
Arrange around turrs in pan:
4 medium potatoes, quartered
4 medium carrots, quartered
1 small turnip, cut in pieces
1 onion, quartered

Continue baking (covered) for 1 hour or until vegetables are tender. Add one can of heated mushrooms.

Mrs. Victoria Gates
Brookfield

Fisherman's Brewis

2 cups fat pork
1 package fillets or fresh fish
5 cakes hard bread (soaked in cold water overnight)

Fry fat pork until a little brown; add fish, cook until you can remove bones; add hard bread, bring to a boil, mash right away and serve. Can be cooked within 30 minutes.

Marilyn J. Glavine
Bishop's Falls

Salmon Roll
with Egg Sauce

2 cups flour
4 tablespoons baking powder
½ teaspoon salt
1 egg
½ cup milk
4 tablespoons shortening
1 large tin salmon
4 tablespoons milk
2 tablespoons lemon juice
1½ tablespoons chopped parsley
½ teaspoon salt

Sift together flour, baking powder, salt and add shortening. Mix well with fork. Beat egg slightly and add milk to make ¾ cup. Add to first mixture. Roll out on floured board to size of 8 inches long, ¼ inch thick. Mix rest of ingredients and spread evenly on dough. Roll as for Jelly Roll and place on a greased baking sheet. Bake in 400° - 425° oven for 30 minutes.

EGG SAUCE
Make 2 cups of white sauce and add 2 chopped hard-boiled eggs and 2 teaspoons finely chopped parsley. Mix and serve hot over salmon roll.

Mrs. James Matthews
Port-aux-Basques

Barbecued Caribou Ribs

3 pounds caribou ribs, cut in pieces
1 cup catsup
2 tablespoons vinegar
2 tablespoons brown sugar
1 teaspoon salt
¼ pound salt pork, diced
1 tablespoon prepared mustard
2 tablespoons lemon juice
1 onion, chopped
¼ teaspoon pepper

Brown ribs in salt pork. Place in casserole and cover with barbecue sauce. Bake at 325 degrees for 2½ hours. Baste sauce over ribs frequently. Delicious served with rice.

Mrs. Elsie Vokey
Gander

Salt Fish Dinner
with Drawn Butter

Water salt fish (if pieces large) about 24 hours changing water often. Boil fish 15 minutes. In separate pot cook potatoes and dumplings. Serve with drawn butter as given below.
Drawn Butter Sauce:
2 boiled onions
¼ cup butter
1 tablespoon corn starch or flour
2 cups boiled water.
Combine butter and flour, add onions and liquid. Heat until thickened. Serve hot with fish and potatoes.

Marilyn J. Glavine
Bishop's Falls

Baked Seal Meat

Remove all fat from about 4 lbs. of seal meat. Soak for 3 hours in
3 cups hot water
1½ teaspoons baking soda
¼ cup vinegar.
Drain seal meat and refrigerate overnight.
Preheat oven to 300°.
Roll meat in a mixture of
1 cup flour
1 teaspoon salt.
Place in roaster with slices of fat pork or butter. Pour over meat the juice of 1 lemon and ¼ cup rum. Cover and roast for 3 hours adding water after first hour of cooking. Make a paste of 3 tablespoons of flour and 1 or 1½ cups cold water, stir into drippings in pan to make a gravy.
Makes about 8 servings.

Mrs. P. Gillingham
Victoria Cove

Quick Onion Rings

Cut large onions in 1/4 inch slices. Separate and dip in Carnation Milk. Coat well with flour and fry in deep fat until golden brown.

Mrs. Frank LeDrew
Pasadena

Balogna Cups

Slice bologna 1/2 inch thick. Remove skin and boil for two or three minutes — slices will curl to form cups. Fill with potatoe salad and serve with lettuce and sliced tomatoes.

Mrs. Frank LeDrew
Pasadena

Moose Pot Pie

2 pounds moose meat
½ cup flour
2 teaspoons salt
Fat pork
4 cups water
6 carrots
2 onions
1 small turnip
3 parsnips
6 potatoes

Cut moose into small cubes, roll into ½ cup flour and 2 teaspoons salt until meat is well coated. Place in a dutch oven with a little fat pork and brown. Then add 4 cups of water and simmer for 2 hours. Add onions & vegetables leaving potatoes for the last. Cook for 25 minutes or until vegetables are done. Cover with pastry and bake for 15 minutes in a 425° oven.

Carrie Mercer
Sunnyside

Moose Stew

3 lbs. moose, cut in small pieces
¼ lb. butter
6 cups water
salt and pepper

Brown moose meat in hot butter, add water, salt and pepper. Let simmer, adding chopped onion after about an hour of cooking. Cook for another hour. Then cut up and add
2 carrots
2 parsnips
1 small turnip
10 potatoes
Cook for 30 minutes or until vegetables are tender. Make dumplings if you wish.

Goldie Stockley
Durrell

Salads

Macaroni Salad

¾ cup mayonnaise
2 tbsp. vinegar
1 tbsp. prepared mustard
1 tsp. sugar
½ tsp. salt
⅛ tsp. pepper
1 pk. (8 oz.) macaroni, (2 cups cooked, drained
    and cooled`
1½ cups chopped celery (or combination of celery,
green & red pepper)
½ cup sliced green onion
¼ cup sweet pickle relish

In large bowl combine mayonnaise, vinegar, mustard,
sugar, salt and pepper and mix well with remaining
ingredients. Cover and chill several hours. Toss before
serving. Makes 8 servings.

Mrs. H. Budgell
St. John's

Cranberry Jelly Salad

1 pk. raspberry jelly
2 cups boiling water
½ cup cranberry crushed
1 med can crushed pineapple with juice
½ cup sugar

Mix sugar with water and jelly. Pour into mold and
chill.

Mrs. H. Budgell
St. John's

Lobster Salad

2 cups cooked, flaked lobster
1 cup finely diced apples
1 cup diced celery
½ cup shredded carrots
2 hard boiled eggs, chopped
½ teaspoon salt
½ cup boiled salad dressing
lettuce
lemon slices

Toss all ingredients except lettuce and lemon slices. Chill and serve on crisp lettuce. Garnish with lemon slices. Serves 6.

Mrs. Kay Fleming
Gander

Partridgeberry Salad

1 package strawberry jelly
1 cup boiling water
2 cups partridgeberries
2 medium sized apples (diced)
¾ cup white sugar

Dissolve jelly in boiling water and chill until partially set. Mix berries and apples with sugar and stir in jelly. Chill and serve.

Eve Russell
Winter Brook
Bonavista Bay

Newfoundland Lobster Salad

3 freshly boiled lobsters (shelled)
½ cup mayonnaise
1 small minced onion
3 hard cooked eggs (chopped)
½ cup sweet pickles (chopped)
½ teaspoon salt
Pinch of pepper

Cut lobster into bite size pieces and toss with above ingredients. Serve on lettuce leaves.

Mrs. Kevin Smith
Elliotts Cove

Salmon Salad

2 cups salmon
3 hard boiled eggs
½ cup diced cheese
3 medium tomatoes, diced, salt to taste
1½ cups macaroni
¼ cup diced sweet pickles
2 tablespoons sweet pickle juice
½ cup diced celery
¾ cup mayonnaise

Mix thoroughly and chill.

Emma Northcott
Lewisporte

Two More Delightful Ideas.

Cabbage Pickles

1 quart cabbage
1 quart vinegar
1 teaspoon salt
1 tablespoon dry mustard
½ cup water
1 quart onions
1 cup white sugar
1 tablespoon curry powder
½ cup flour

Chop cabbage and onions fine. Add vinegar and boil for 10 minutes. Add sugar & salt. Mix seasonings with flour adding enough water to make a paste. Stir paste into boiling pickles and boil for 20 minutes. Bottle and seal while hot.

Rita Babstock
Clarenville

Lobster Stuffed Eggs

6 hard boiled eggs
1 cup cooked lobster
1 teaspoon prepared mustard
2 teaspoons mayonnaise
Salt & pepper
Paprika

Cut eggs in half and remove the yolks. In a bowl yolks and mix in lobster, mustard, mayonnaise an. seasonings. Spoon into boiled egg whites and sprinkle top with paprika. Chill and serve.

Mrs. Roy Warren
North West Brook
Trinity Bay

Partridgeberry Bread

2 cups sifted all purpose Flour
½ teaspoon salt
1½ teaspoons baking powder
½ teaspoon baking soda
2 tablespoons butter
1 cup white sugar
1 egg
1 orange juiced with grated rind (keep separated)
boiling water
1 cup walnuts chopped
1 cup raw partridgeberries

Sift flour, salt, baking powder and soda twice. Cream butter adding sugar and beat well. Add beaten eggs to sugar and butter mixture. Add enough boiling water to orange juice to make ¾ cup liquid. Add dry ingredients alternately with liquid to the creamed mixture. Add grated orange rind, walnuts and berries mixing thoroughly. Pour batter into a greased loaf pan and let rise for 10 minutes. Bake for 50-60 minutes in a 325° Oven.

Mrs. Amy Batten
Terra Nova

Blueberry Bread

2 eggs
1 cup sour milk
½ cup brown sugar
⅓ cup salad oil
1 cup rolled oats
2 cups flour
1 teaspoon baking powder
1 teaspoon baking soda
1 teaspoon salt
½ teaspoon nutmet
1 cup chopped nuts
1½ cups blueberries.

Preheat oven to 350°. Grease 9 x 5 x 3 loaf pan. Beat eggs, stir in milk, brown sugar, salad oil and rolled oats. Sift flour, baking powder, soda, salt, and nutmeg together. Stir into mixture just enough to blend. Add nuts and blueberries and fold just enough to blend them through batter. Spoon into pan. Spread evenly. Bake for one hour. Cool a few minutes before turning out on cake rack. Wrap in aluminum foil to store.

Alison H. Bartle
Grand Falls

Pork Buns

1 cup salt fat back pork
½ cup boiling water
2½ cups flour
2 teaspoons baking powder
½ cup molasses

Cut pork into very small pieces. Add the molasses to the boiling water and pour over the pork. Sift flour and baking powder together and add to first mixture. Mix together lightly. Pour into greased muffin pans and bake 25 to 30 minutes in a moderate oven.

Mrs. James Green
Carbonear

Old-Fashioned Sweet Bread

2 pks. yeast
1 cup lukewarm water
2 teaspoons sugar
2 tablespoons butter
4 teaspoons salt
3 teaspoons caraway seeds
12 cups flour
3 cups raisins
1 cup molasses

Dissolve yeast in 1 cup lukewarm water to which sugar has been added. Combine 3 cups lukewarm water, molasses, & butter. Sift dry ingredients together and add raisins & carraway seeds. Mix well and add to liquid ingredients. Knead dough and let rise until double in bulk. Knead and let rise again until double in bulk. Shape dough and place in greased loaf pans to rise. Bake in 375° oven for 1 hour.

Mrs. Vicki Hewitt
Lewisporte

Tea Buns

3 cups flour
3 heaping teaspoons baking powder
⅓ cup sugar
Pinch of salt
½ cup butter
1 tablespoon lard
1 egg, slightly beaten
1 cup water

Sift dry ingredients together and rub in butter and lard. Mix with egg and water. Do not over mix. Roll out and cut buns. Bake for 20 minutes in a 450° oven.

Mrs. Kenneth Randell
Shoal Harbour

Molasses Pudding

2½ cups flour
1 teaspoon baking soda
½ teaspoon salt (omit if pork is used)
1 teaspoon mixed spice
½ cup butter or 1 cup suet (cut fine) or ½ cup salt pork
(cut fine).
1 cup molasses
1 cup milk or water
1 cup raisins
1 cup currants (optional)
⅓ cup peel (optional)

Sift flour, soda, salt, and spice. Add molasses and milk
(or water). Add fruit coated with flour and butter. Mix
well. Steam for 2½ hours boiling constantly. Serve with
a sauce.

Dorothy Drodge
Adeyton,
Trinity Bay

Bread Pudding

4 eggs slightly beaten
½ cup sugar
3 cups heated milk
2 tablespoons butter
2 teaspoons vanilla
½ cup crushed pineapple with juice
2 cups soft bread crumbs
Pinch of salt

Combine eggs, sugar and salt in a bowl. Slowly stir in
hot milk and butter. Mix and add vanilla, pineapple and
bread crumbs. Pour into baking dish and place dish in a
pan of hot water. Bake for 1¼ hours in 350° oven.

Frances Williams
Corner Brook

Nfld. Partridgeberry Bread

2 cups flour
1 cup light brown sugar
1 teaspoon baking powder
1 teaspoon baking soda
½ cup margarine or butter
2 eggs - well beaten
Rind and juice of one orange
1 cup light raisins
1½ cups partridgeberries

Place flour, sugar, baking powder, baking soda in deep
pan, mix with spoon. Crumble butter or margarine with
flour mixture by hand. Add raisins, beaten eggs,
orange rind and juice. Add partridgeberries last. Bake
at 350 degrees for one hour or when straw inserted in
middle is dry.

Mrs. Frank LeDrew
Pasadena

Molasses Buns

1 cup molasses
1 cup melted butter
1 egg
½ cup milk
4½ cups flour
1 cup sugar
2 teaspoons ginger
2 teaspoons cloves (chopped)
2 teaspoons baking soda
pinch of salt

Add melted butter to molasses and stir. Add milk and
egg. Stir. Mix in remaining ingredients. Roll out on a
floured board to ½ inch thickness. Cut in desired shapes
and place on greased cookie sheet. Bake in 400° oven for
15-20 minutes.

Mrs. Philip Pritchett
Bishop's Falls

Figgy Duff

½ cup butter
2 cups flour
1 egg
¾ cup sugar
2 teaspoons baking powder
½ cup milk or water
1 cup raisins
Pinch of salt

Combine dry ingredients and add milk and egg. Place in cloth bag and boil for 1 hour in pot of water. Ingredients can also be steamed in a pudding mold. To make a plain duff follow same recipe but omit raisins.

Mrs. Olive Paul
Bonavista

Bangbelly
A Traditional Christmas Eve Dish.

3 cups cooked rice
1 cup flour
1 cup molasses
2 cups raisins
1¼ cups salt pork (cubed)
1½ teaspoons baking soda
1 teaspoon baking powder
1 teaspoon cinnamon
½ teaspooon all spice
¼ teaspoon cloves
¼ teaspoon mixed spice

Allow rice to cool and add salt pork and molasses. Sift together flour and spices. Add raisins, mixing all ingredients together. Pour into 9'' x 9'' greased pans. Bake for 1¼ hours in a 350° oven.

Mrs. Annie Noble
Lewisporte

Cranberry Bread

⅓ cup shortening
2 eggs
1¼ cups sugar
2¼ cups flour
1½ teaspoons baking powder
1 teaspoon baking soda
1 teaspoon salt
1 cup raw cranberries (cut)
¾ cup chopped walnuts
Grated rind and juice of 1 orange

Squeeze juice of orange and put in measuring cup. Fill cup with hot water. Add this mixture to shortening and set aside to cool. Beat eggs until thick and gradually beat in sugar.
Alternately add dry ingredients and orange juice mixture. Fold in combined cranberries, orange rind and nuts. Shape dough and place in greased loaf pans and bake in 350° oven for 1 hour.

Myrtle Mouland
Bonavista

Nfld. Pork Buns

3 cups of Cream of the West flour
5 teaspoon baking powder
½ lb. salt pork, cut small
½ cup shortening
1 cup cold water
1½ cups raisins

Mix in order given. Bake at 375°.

Mrs. Myrtle Bennett
Channel

Pineapple Cake

1 pound butter
1 pound sugar
5 eggs
4 cups flour
1 teaspoon baking powder
1 teaspoon vanilla
1 cup milk
½ pound dates
1 pound raisins
1 pound currants
½ teaspoon salt
½ pound mixed peel
1 tin crushed (strained pineapple)
1 cup coconut
½ cup cherries

Method: Cream butter and sugar, add beaten eggs, coconut and fruit, add milk. Sift baking powder, flour and salt together, add to first mixture, add pineapple. Bake four hours in a slow oven, 250 degrees.

Gladys Howell
St. John's

Dark Fruit Cake

½ pound butter
1 cup brown sugar
1 cup molasses
4 eggs, beaten
2 cups flour
1 teaspoon baking powder
1 teaspoon soda
½ teaspoon ginger
1 teaspoon cinnamon
1 teaspoon allspice
½ teaspoon cloves
2 teaspoons cocoa
½ pound cherries
½ pounds nuts
½ pound dates
1 pound raisins
1 pound currants
½ pound mixed fruit
2 apples, cut fine
½ cup red jam
1 cup milk
2 teaspoons coffee mixed with ½ cup water
1 teaspoon vanilla, rum and lemon flavouring

Sift dry ingredients. Mix fruits and dredge with flour. Cream butter and sugar. Add eggs and molasses, add flour to creamed mixture with milk and coffee. Add fruit last. Blend mixture well so that all fruit will be well covered with batter. Pour batter in whatever size pan you wish and bake at 275° to 300° for 2½ to 3 hours, depending on the size of pan used.

Emma Northcott
Lewisporte

Apple Crumble Desert

⅔ cup flour
¾ cup brown sugar, packed
⅓ cup butter
4 cups sliced apples

Combine flour, sugar and cut in butter to make a crumbly mixture. Arrange sliced apples into prepared baking dish. Sprinkle sugar mixture over top. Sprinkle with cinnamon and bake 375 degrees about 30 minutes or until top is brown and crunchy. Serve with ice cream or whipped cream.

Mrs. Elsie Vokey
Gander

─────

Blueberry Crisp

Ingredients:

3 cups blueberries
⅔ cup sugar
1 tbsp. flour
3 tbsp. butter or margarine
¼ cup brown sugar
¼ cup sifted flour
¾ cup rolled oats.

Method: Place blueberries in greased baking dish and sprinkle with ⅔ cups sugar and 1 tbsp. flour. Cream margarine, add brown sugar and cream well together. Blend in flour and rolled oats to make a crumb mixture. Sprinkle this crumb mixture on top of the blueberries. Bake in a moderately hot oven 375°F. until the blueberries are soft and the top is golden brown, about 40 minutes.

Priscilla March
Lady Cove

Candlelight Fruit Cake

Oven temperature - 325°F, pre-heated. Well grease and lightly flour one 10-inch tube cake pan.

1 cup butter or margarine
2 cups sugar
4 eggs
4 cups Cream of the West flour
1½ teaspoons baking soda
1½ cups sour milk
1½ cups walnut or pecan pieces
1½ cups chopped dates
¾ cup cliced candied cherries
¾ cup diced candied pineapple
¼ cup freshly grated orange peel
1¼ cups sugar
2 tablespoons lemon juice
2 tablespoons grated orange peel
1 cup fresh orange juice.

Cream butter or margarine, gradually add sugar and beat until light and fluffy. Add eggs, one at a time, beating after each addition. Beat in 1 cup Cream of the West flour. use ½ cup of flour quantity to coat nuts and fruit, then set aside. Stir baking soda into sour milk, add to creamed mixture alternately with remaining flour, beating until smooth. Stir in flour-coated nuts, fruit and ¼ cup orange peel. Place in prepared 10-inch tube pan. Bake at 325° for 2 hours or until cake tests done. To prevent over-browning, place a piece of aluminum foil on top of the cake during the last 45 minutes of baking. Cool on wire rack 10 minutes. Meanwhile combine remaining ingredients in saucepan; briskly boil one minute. Remove cake from pan. Pierce entire surface with fork or sharp instrument. Slowly spoon hot syrup over cake until all syrup is absorbed. Stores well in refrigerator if tightly wrapped in aluminum foil.

Mrs. Seymour Gates
Brookfield

Rhubarb Upside Down Cake

Oven 350° Time: 1 hour or less

3 cups sliced rhubarb
1½ Cups miniature marshmallows
1¾ Cups sugar
½ Cup Crisco
2 Eggs
¼ tsp. salt
1 tbsp. baking powder
½ Cup milk
¾ Cups flour

Place rhubarb, marshmallows and ¾ cup sugar in 7'' x 11'' glass cake pan. Cream shortening and remaining sugar, add eggs and beat well. Add flour, salt and baking powder. Add alternately with milk. Pour batter over rhubarb. Bake for 1 hour or less depending on oven. Cool for 5 minutes. Invert on serving plate. DO NOT DOUBLE RECIPE.

Mrs. N. Riggs
Glovertown

Partridgeberry Tart

Pastry:
    2 cups flour
1 teaspoon baking powder
½ teaspoon salt
½ cup icing sugar
7/8 cup shortening
1 egg
1 tablespoon milk
Stir dry ingredients together and work in shortening. Add beaten egg and milk. Roll out and place half pastry in 9'' pie plate. Fill with partidgebery jam and top with remaining pastry. Bake in 400° oven until golden brown. To keep edges from burning make a ''collar'' by cutting foil to fit. Remove later.

Alison H. Bartle
Grand Falls

Trifle

2 jelly or jam rolls. (sliced)
1 pkg. of frozen strawberry halves. (thawed)
½ cup of orange juice.
¼ cup of sherry.
2 cups of (prepared) vanilla custard.
1 pkg. of strawberry flavored jello powder.
1 tin of whipped carnation milk.

Step 1: Prepare strawberry flavored jello powder as directed on the package, and put aside to set well.
Step 2: Prepare vanilla custard...using a double boiler arrange 1 cup of scald milk. Add 1 beaten egg, 1 teaspoon of sugar, ½ teaspoon vanilla and a speck of salt. Bring this to a boil stirring constantly, until thick and smooth. Set aside to cool.
Step 3: Into a large glass dish arrange (some) jelly or jam roll slices laying them flat around the sides of the dish. Add a little of your (set) jello in the bottom and between each jelly roll slice. Add a strawberry half here and there and sprinkle a little orange juice and sherry on each slice. Begin again with jelly or jam slices over-lapping each one around the sides and bottom of dish, sprinkle with orange juice and sherry, and continue with the jello and strawberry halves. Pour some of your prepared vanilla custard around each piece of jelly roll slice allowing it to run free through the dish preparations. Continue alternately with jelly slices, jello, vanilla custard and strawberry halves (strawberry juice too) and the sherry etc. until all ingredients are used up, to fill your dish.
Step 4: Whip 1 tin of carnation milk and spread on top ..garnish with strawberries.

Laura Francis
Glenwood

Old Fashioned Blueberry Cake

½ cup sugar
1 cup butter
1 egg
1 cup molasses
1 tsp. vanilla
4 cups flour
1 tsp soda
1¼ cups milk
3½ cups blueberries
1 teaspoon each cloves, cinnamon, nutmet and allspice

Method: Cream butter and sugar, add egg and beat well. Add vanilla and mollasses. Add sifted dry ingredients alternately with milk. Finally add blueberries which have been dredged with flour.
Bake 1½ hours in 350° oven in two loaf pans if desired.

Goldie Stockley
Durrell

Cherry Squares

½ cup butter
½ cup shortening
2½ cups brown sugar
3 eggs
3 cups flour
3 teaspoons baking powder
3 teaspoons almond flavouring
1 cup sliced cherries
1 cup walnuts
½ teaspoon salt

Cream sugar and shortening together. Add eggs first, then, dry ingredients. Mix in fruit. Spread in 9 x 13'' cake pan. Bake for 20 minutes at 350°. Cut into squares while warm.

Mrs. Shirley Wareham
Carbonear

Rhubarb-and-Carrot Marmalade

4 cups carrots
4 cups rhubarb
2 oranges
2 lemons
6 cups sugar
1½ cups water

Peel carrots. Wash and dry rhubarb, oranges and lemons. Cut rhubarb in ½ inch lengths. Shred carrots, oranges and lemons very thinly. Combine all ingredients and bring to boil, stirring to prevent scorching. Boil for 1 hour. Pour into hot sterilized jars and seal.

Miss Grace Percy
Brigus
Conception Bay
Newfoundland

Bakeapple Crumbles

Boil 1 quart bakeapples in water until soft and thick. Add sugar to sweeten.

2 cups flour
1 cup butter
2 cups rolled oats
2 teaspoons cinnamon
1 cup sugar

Combine above ingredients and cover the bottom of a greased pan with half the mixture. Spread with bakeapple mixture and top with remaining dry ingredients. Bake in moderate oven until brown.

Cindi MacAdam
Elliotts Cove
Trinity Bay

Old Fashioned Blueberry Cake

3 cups all purpose Flour
3 teaspoons baking powder
¼ teaspoon baking soda
¼ teaspoon salt
3 cups blueberries (fresh or frozen)
2 teaspoons allspice
2 teaspoons cinnamon
½ cup sugar
1 cup salt pork (cut in small cubes)
1 cup molasses
1½ cups water

Mix the first nine ingredients into a large bowl. Set aside. Stir the molasses into the water and gradually fold into the flour mixture until thoroughly blended. Place into a greased 10'' x 10'' baking pan and bake at 350° for 1 hour or until golden brown. Serve hot or cold.

NOTE: This cake is delicious served hot with roasted fish.

Mrs. Alexander Over
Southern Bay
B. Bay

Jam Jams

1 cup butter
1 egg
½ cup sugar
½ cup molasses
2 tsp. baking soda dissolved in 3 tablespoons of boiling water.
Enough flour to make a soft dough

Roll and cut out with cookie cutters. Bake 10-12 minutes. While hot spread with jam and place two together.

Mrs. Blanche Pink
Ramea

Blueberry Upside-Down Pudding

1½ cups flour
3 tsp. baking powder
¾ cup sugar
½ teaspoon salt
¾ cup milk
¼ cup margarine
1 egg, slightly beaten.

Sift flour, sugar, baking powder and salt. Cut in margarine. Make hollow in middle of mixture and add milk mixed with egg. Combine until moistened well. Spread this mixture over the following:
2 cups blueberries
1 teaspoon lemon rind
½ cup sugar
which has been combined and spread in the dish. Bake 45-50 minutes in 350° oven.
Partridgeberries may be used instead of blueberries with more sugar and no lemon rind.

Alison H. Bartle
Grand Falls

Quickie Squares

1 cup margarine
1 cup brown sugar
1 teaspoon baking powder
2 cups crushed graham wafers
1 teaspoon vanilla
1 cup milk
1 egg
1 cup coconut

Mix all ingredients together and bake in a square pan (greased) at 325 degrees for 30 minutes. When cool cut in squares. Top with plain white icing. Garnish with raisins, cherries or currants if desired.

Mrs. Frank LeDrew
Pasadena

Tweed Squares

½ cup butter
⅔ cup brown sugar
½ cup milk
1⅓ cups flour
2 teaspoons baking powder
pinch salt
2 squares semi-sweet chocolate, grated
2 eggs.

Cream butter, sugar, salt and vanilla, then add flour, baking powder and milk, then grated chocolate last of all. Fold in egg whites beaten stiffly. Put in 9 x 9 inch pan and bake 30 minutes on 325° oven.
Topping:
2 tablespoons butter, 2 egg yolks, creamed together. Add enough icing sugar to make a stiff icing. Spread over top when cold, then melt 2 tablespoons butter, 2 squares semi-sweet chocolate together and pour over icing mixture. Put in fridge a few minutes until chocolate hardens.
Cut into squares

Mrs. Doris Gosse
Corner Brook

Boiled Raisin Cake

1 pkg. raisins
3 cups cold water
2 cups sugar
½ pound butter
1 teaspoons cinnamon and cloves

Boil for 20 minutes and cool. Mix 1 teaspoon soda in water and add to cold mixture. Then add 4 cups flour, 1 teaspoon salt and 1 teaspoon baking powder. Bake about 2 hours.

Jean Rice
Windsor

Dark Fruit Cake

3½ cups Flour
1 cup Molasses
1 cup Sugar
1 cup Butter
1 pkg. Raisins
1 pkg. Currants
1 pkg. Mixed Fruit
1 pkg. Cherries
5 Eggs
1 tsp. Cinnamon
1 tsp. Cloves
½ tsp. Salt
1 tbsp. Allspice
1 tsp. Soda dissolved in 2 tbsp. Hot Water
1 wineglass full of Pineapple Flavouring or Rum

Steep spices in molasses over low heat. DO NOT BOIL. The longer it steeps the darker the cake will be. Cream butter, sugar, well-beaten eggs and cool molasses mixture. Dust fruit with ½ cup flour. Add remaining flour and salt to the butter mixture. Blend well. Stir in flavoured fruit. Lastly, mix in soda dissolved in hot water. Use a large baking pan. Bake at 375 degrees for 3 to 3½ hours.

Mrs. Irene Churchill
Hare Bay

O-Henry Cookies

1 cup brown sugar
½ cup milk
½ cup butter
Bring to a boil, remove from heat and add 1 cup crushed Graham wafers, 1 cup coconut and ½ cup chopped nuts. Put into a 9 x 12 inch greased pan which has whole wafers on bottom, lay another layer of wafers on top and press down gently. Ice with chocolate icing.

Jean Rice
Windsor

Partridgeberry Pie

2 cups all-purpose flour
1 cup margarine (Good Luck)
⅓ cup milk
1 teaspoon vinegar added to milk
1½ to 2 cups berries
sugar and butter

Pastry:
   Mix flour and margarine with pastry blender until it resembles crumbs, add the milk mixture, a little at a time, stirring with a fork or knife.
Roll out on slightly floured board and cut to fit pie plate, put in amount of berries required and sprinkle with sugar to taste, add a few small pieces of Good Luck. Cover with strips or full size layer of pastry.
Bake in hot oven.
Makes two small double pies or one large one.

Mrs. F.W. Baker
Botwood

Rhubarb Crumble Pie

½ cup melted butter
½ cup sifted flour
1½ cups rolled oats
1½ tablespoon flour
⅔ cup brown sugar
3 cups raw rhubarb
½ cup white sugar

Combine melted butter, rolled oats, flour and brown sugar. Firmly press ¾ of the mixture into a 9 inch pie plate and cover with rhubarb. Combine the 1½ cups sugar and 1½ tablespoons flour. Sprinkle this over the rhubarb and top with remaining crumbs. Bake for 45 minutes in a 350° oven. Top with cream, if desired.

Joyce Martin
Trepassey
Southern Shore

Lemon & Currant Loaf

½ lb. butter
1½ cups sugar
3 eggs
3½ cups flour
2 tsp. baking powder
1 tsp. vanilla
1 cup milk
1 pkg. currants
Rind and juice of 1 lemon

Cream butter and sugar well, add eggs one at a time and beat well. Combine flour and baking powder, add to butter mixture alternately with milk, add lemon juice, rind and vanilla. Fold in currants. Bake for two hrs. at 250 to 300°. Makes two loaves.

Marie Cull
St. John's

Dutch Dainties

½ cup butter or margarine
½ cup brown sugar
1 egg yoke
1 cup flour
1 tsp. vanilla
⅛ tsp. soda

Cream butter and sugar, add egg yoke and beat; add flour and soda sifted together, a tsp. of milk may be needed to make soft dough. Pinch off little bits and press into patty pans.

Filling:
1 egg white stiffly beaten
½ cup brown sugar
¼ cup coconut
¼ cup walnuts (chopped fine)
¼ cup cherries (chopped)
Pinch of baking powder

Mix all together, put small amount into patty shells and bake in a fairly quick oven.

Statia Underhay
St. John's

45

Date-Nut Squares

½ cup soft butter
¼ cup icing sugar
1 cup flour
1 egg
¼ cup granulated sugar
1 package (3¼ ounces) coconut cream pudding and pie filling mix
½ cup undiluted Carnation Evaporated Milk.
1⅔ cups flaked coconut
½ cup chopped nuts
½ cup chopped dates

In mixer bowl, cream butter with icing sugar until light and fluffy. Gradually add flour. Beat for 2 minutes at medium speed. Press evenly into buttered 8-inch square pan. Bake in moderate oven (350 degrees) for about 15 minutes. Beat egg. Gradually beat in granulated sugar. Stir in pudding mix, baking powder, evaporated milk, coconut, nuts and dates. Spread over hot crust. Bake for about 30 minutes. Cool thoroughly. Cut into 16 squares with a very sharp knife. Dip knife in hot water for easier cutting.

Mrs. Frank LeDrew
Pasadena

Jelly Roll

3 large eggs
1 cup sugar
½ tsp. lemon extract
1 cup flour
¼ tsp. salt
1 tsp. baking powder
1 table spoon cold water

Separate eggs, beat yokes until thick, gradually adding sugar, add lemon extract, then stir in the stiffly beaten whites, fold flour, baking powder and salt, which have been sifted together (five times) add cold water. Line shallow pan with well greased wax paper. Bake 12 mins. Sprinkle damp towel with sugar, turn sponge out on this, cut strips from sides and ends. Spread with jam, roll up, quickly wrap in wax paper until cool.

Statia Underhay
St. John's

Ginger Bread

¼ cup shortening
2 tablespoons sugar
¾ cup boiling water
1 egg
1 cup molasses
1 tsp. soda
1 tsp. salt
1 tsp. ginger
½ tsp. cinnamon
1¾ cup flour

Pour water over shortening, beat sugar into beaten egg, add salt and spices to flour, add molasses beat again. Bake in quick oven for 20 mins.

Statia Underhay
St. John's

Light Fruit Cake

½ lb. margarine
1½ cup sugar
3 eggs
3½ cups flour
1 teaspoon baking powder
1 cup milk
1 lb. raisins
1 lb. mixed peel
1 tsp. lemon flavouring
1 tsp. vanilla
Pinch of salt

Cream margarine, add sugar a little at a time to margarine, add eggs and beat well. Sift flour, salt and baking powder together, add flavouring to creamed mixture. Then flour mixture with milk, add fruit, bake in slow oven for about 2 hrs. or until cake is done when tested.

Statia Underhay
St. John's

Newfoundland Seven Cup Pudding

1 cup chopped apple
1 cup hard beef suet (chopped fine)
1 cup all-purpose flour
1 cup white sugar
1 cup bread crumbs
1 cup dark raisins
1 cup carnation milk
¼ teaspoon soda.

Put all seven cups of ingredients into a mixing bowl, and let stand over night. Then add ¼ teaspoon baking soda and mix together well. Pour into a well greased pudding mold and steam for 3 hours. Serve hot with lemon sauce or a thin custard sauce.
This mixture will appear very white, but will come out a rich dark texture when steamed properly. It can be prepared and kept for weeks...re-steam for 1 hr. when needed.

Mrs. Laura Francis
Glenwood

Steamed Blueberry Pudding

Mix together:
    ½ cup butter
    ½ cup brown sugar
    ½ cup molasses
Add:
    ½ cup hot water
    1 teaspoon soda
    1 teaspoon cinnamon
    Enough flour for stiff dough. Add 2 cups blueberries.
Steam for 2 hours.

Mrs. Elsie Vokey
Gander

Partridgeberry Bars

Preheat oven to 375°. Grease an 8'' sq. cake pan.
Combine:—
      1 cup flour
      1 cup lightly packed brown sugar
      1 cup rolled oats
Cut in until crumbly - ½ cup butter or margarine.
Press half into prepared pan. Spread with 1½ cups partridgeberry jam. Cover with remaining crumbs and pat smooth.
Bake at 375° for 35 minutes or until lightly browned.
Cool and cut into bars. Can be served hot with ice cream.

Mrs. Marion Collins
Hare Bay, B. Bay

Crunchy Partridgeberry Tarts

6 unbaked tart shells (use muffin tins to hold tart shells)
1 cup chopped apple
1 cup partridgeberry jam
1 tablespoon flour
¼ teaspoon nutmeg
¼ teaspoon cinnamon

Mix apple and jam together. Combine flour and spices and stir into jam mixture. Spoon into unbaked tart shells. Spread with topping and bake 425° for 30 minutes.
Crumb Topping:
      ½ cup flour
      ½ cup brown sugar
      ¼ cup butter or margarine
Cut in butter or margarine until mixture is crumby.

Mrs. Mildred Bowdridge
Birchy Bay

Apple Dumplings

Pastry
Stir together 2½ cups cake and pastry flour
¾ cup plus 1 tablespoon shortening
1¼ tsp. salt
3 tbsp. butter
2½ tbsp. cold water

Filling
6 medium size apples, pared and cored
¼ cup sugar
¾ teaspoon cinnamon

Syrup
¼ cup lemon juice
1 cup sugar
¾ cup water
3 tablespoons margarine.

Method: Make pastry by cutting shortening and butter into the flour and salt until pieces are very small. Drizzle in water and toss with fork until pastry can be easily handled. Roll out on floured board and cut into six squares. Place an apple on each square and fill with cinnamon and sugar (mixed tog.) Wrap each apple in pastry and pinch to seal. Prick with fork in two or three places. Place in greased baking pan (2 ins. apart). Bake at 450° for 20 minutes.

Into small pot put lemon juice, margarine, sugar and water. Bring just to boil. Spoon over apples and reduce heat to 350° for 15 minutes or until apples are tender when tested with skewer. Serve hot with cream.

Mrs. H. Budgell
St. John's

Quick Holiday Fruit Cake

1 pkg. date bar mix
⅔ cup hot water
3 eggs
¼ cup flour
¾ teaspoon baking powder
1 teaspoon cinnamon
¼ teaspoon nutmeg
¼ teaspoon allspice
1 cup coarsely chopped nuts
1 cup candied cherries
1 cup cut-up dried appricots
½ cup cut-up candied pineapple
Apple Jelly Glaze (see below)

Heat oven to 325°. Grease and flour loaf pan, 9 x 5 x 3 inches. Blend date filling from date mix package and hot water. Add crumbly mix, eggs, flour, baking powder and spices, mix thoroughly. Stir in nuts, cherries, apricots and pineapple. Spread mixture evenly in pan. Bake 1 hour and 20 minutes or until wooden pick instered in center comes out clean. Cool thoroughly. Wrap in plastic wrap or aluminum foil, refrigerage. Glaze cake just before serving.

Apple Jelly Glaze:
Heat ¼ cup apple or currant jelly over low heat until smooth, stirring occasionally. Spoon over cake.

Shirley Gates
Brookfield

Frozen Spiced Crab Apples

16 small ripe crab apples
1 cup sugar
1 cup water
½ cup red cinnamon candies
3 pieces lemon peel, cut in 1½ x ¼ inch strips
6 whole cloves
¼ teaspoon ground ginger
Dash salt

Remove blossom end of crab apples; do not remove stem or peel. In saucepan combine sugar, water, red cinnamon candies, lemon peel, whole cloves, ground ginger and salt; bring to boiling. Prick apples in several places and place, stem up, in boiling mixture. Return to boiling; reduce heat. Cover; cook over low heat 10 minutes. Do not stir. Remove from heat; cool apples completely in syrup.
Pick apples up by stems; pack in moisture-proof containers. Strain syrup over apples. Seal, label, and freeze. Thaw 1 to 2 hours before serving. Makes 16 spiced apples.

Mrs. Verbena Phillips
Grenfell Heights
Grand Falls

Bakeapple Jam

1 pound washed bakeapples
¾ pound white sugar.

Put sugar on berries and let stand overnight. Next day put on to cook, bringing the jam slowly to a boil. Boil 20-30 minutes. Pour immediately into sterilized hot jars and seal.

Marilyn Glavine
Bishop's Falls

Coffee Cake

2 tablespoons butter, melted
¾ cup brown sugar
1 teaspoon cinnamon
1 ¾ cups flour
3 teaspoons baking powder
½ teaspoon salt
⅔ cup sugar
⅓ cup shortening
1 egg
1 cup milk
½ teaspoon vanilla

Preheat oven to moderate, 375°F. Grease thoroughly an 8'' x 8'' pan.
Melt 2 tablespoons butter. Stir in the brown sugar and cinnamon. Set aside for top of coffee cake.
Measure flour without sifting into large mixing bowl; add baking powder, salt, and sugar and stir thoroughly to blend.
Cut in the shortening with pastry blender.
Make a hollow and add egg, milk and vanilla. Break egg yolk and stir milk and egg together in hollow; then combine with dry ingredients, mixing just until moistened.
Turn into pan and sprinkle with brown sugar-cinnamon mixture.
Bake in moderate oven 30 to 35 minutes.
Serve warm.

Miss Grace Percy
Brigus,
Conception Bay
Newfoundland

Beverages

Nfld. Egg Nog

1 bottle of Newfoundland Screech
1 quart of fresh milk
1 tin evaporated milk
6 eggs
½ cup white sugar

Seperate eggs and beat yolks with ¼ cup of sugar and whites with ¼ cup of sugar. In large container pour 1 bottle of Newfoundland Screech, 1 quart milk and 1 tin evaporated milk and egg yolk mixture. Beat for about two minutes then top with egg whites. Sprinkle with nut-meg.

Mrs. Frank LeDrew
Pasadena

Dogberry Wine

Place 2 gallons of berries in a boiler with 1 gallon of water. Boil for 2 hours. Press and strain. Place juice back in boiler for 1 hour adding sugar to taste. When cool, strain and bottle.

Mrs. Hilda Earle
Summerford

Newfoundland Punch

2 cups strong tea
1 cup sugar
1 cup orange juice
½ cup lemon juice
1 cup cranberry juice
1 cup pineapple juice
Ginger Ale

Method: Heat tea and sugar until sugar is dissolved.
Add rest of ingredients except ginger ale. Cool. When
ready to serve, add ginger ale to taste. Pour into punch
bowl, adding round or ice made by putting water into a
mold and scattering red and green cherries before
freezing.

Mrs. P. Gillingham
Victoria Cove

Dogberry Wine

1 quart dogberries
1 gallon boiling water
4 pounds sugar plus 1 cup sugar
2 lemons
2 oranges
1 package yeast.

Put berries in open jar, add boiling water then sugar
and sliced fruit. Allow to cool, then add yeast, stirring
thoroughly. After 3 weeks strain and bottle.

Mrs. Phyllis Gillingham
Victoria Cove

Rhubarb Juice

2½ lbs. Rhubarb
2 qts. water
1¼ cup sugar
Juice of two lemons
Juice of one orange
4 whole cloves

Cut rhubarb & stew in simmering water, strain through cheesecloth. Add sugar, lemon, orange juice & cloves, refrigerate and serve while cold.

Mrs. H. Budgell
St. John's

Blueberry Wine

2 quarts blueberries
4 quarts boiling water
6 cups sugar
3 cups prunes

Add boiling water to berries and crush berries. Bring to boil and cook 10 minutes. Strain juice and add 6 cups of sugar to 1 gallon juice. Cool to lukewarm, add prunes and 1 package yeast. Cover with cloth and let stand in a warm place for 2 months. Strain, bottle and cork.

Mrs. Elsie Vokey
Gander